Golden Rules of LBP

1 Keep your head down, do your bird, ride out your bang up.

2 Its nice to be nice, be positive, entertain and see the bright side.

3 Don't believe everything you hear inside HMP.

4 Pay your bills if you borrow.

5 Never lose your cool.

The Little Book of Prison

Published 2012 by

Waterside Press Ltd.

Sherfield Gables

Sherfield on Loddon

Hook, Hampshire

United Kingdon RG27 0JG

Telephone +44(0)1256 882250

Low cost UK landline calls 0845 2300 733

E-mail enquiries@watersidepress.co.uk

Online catalogue WatersidePress.co.uk

ISBN 978-1-904380-83-2 (**Paperback**)   978-1-908162-09-0 (**eBook**)

Cataloguing-In-Publication Data A catalogue record for this book can be obtained on request from the British Library.

Cover design Front cover design by Amber Jefferson-Grant © Waterside Press.

UK distributor Gardners Books, 1 Whittle Drive, Eastbourne, East Sussex, BN23 6QH. Tel: +44 (0)1323 521777; sales@gardners.com; www.gardners.com

North American distributor International Specialized Book Services (ISBS), 920 NE 58th Ave, Suite 300, Portland, Oregon, 97213-3786, USA, Tel: 1 800 944 6190 Fax 1 503 280 8832; orders@isbs.com; www.isbs.com

Printing and binding by CPI Group (UK) Ltd, Croydon, CR0 4YY.

The Little Book
of Prison
A Beginners Guide
Frankie Owens
A1443CA

Contents

Acknowledgements

I would like to thank The Koestler Trust for the award, the late John Sullivan writer of "Only Fools and Horses" fame for his inspiration and Ronnie Barker for his delivery as Norman Stanley Fletcher in "Porridge". As Fletch said, "If you can't do the time, don't do the crime".

Frankie Owens

January 2012

Koestler Platinum Award Winner

Our awards judges don't give a Platinum Award lightly, and this book is a winner on more than one level. It is a practical and totally frank introduction to real life in the British prison system — probably the best introduction there is.

But it is also a wonderfully human narrative and a sharply argued critique — the wit and wisdom of one inmate who turns out to be a born writer. I was gripped from start to finish — roared with laughter one minute, winced with pain the next, and was left wondering why we have prisons at all.

Tim Robertson, Chief Executive, The Koestler Trust

Absolutely hilarious, I'm not sure it'll ever be standard prison issue but maybe it should be! Packed full of witty and wry observations and some extremely pertinent advice. It is well-structured, easy to read and informative. I hope he continues writing as The Little Book of Prison is something that the general public would love to read as well as a guide book for other prisoners

Koestler Award Judges

DEDICATION

This book is dedicated to
Amelia Grace, Sophia May and Megan Rose

"Sorry daddy went away, he missed you every day".

The Little Book of Prison

About the Author

Frankie Owens was prisoner A1443CA "at Her Majesty's pleasure" until 2 August 2011. If he had been given the information gathered together in LBP, he thinks that the first weeks inside would have been better and the learning curve not as steep.

Introduction

I'm a first time offender detained at Her Majesty's pleasure at HMP X a holding prison that is considered one of the hardest to handle. Not because it's full of Category A prisoners but because the rules of bang up are the worst in terms of prisoner liberty. You are locked up 22 hours a day … yep a day!!!! In a 14 ft by 8 ft cell between two of you.

As a first offender you have no idea how the system or a prison works, you are clueless about it all and it is frightening for both the person going in and the family and loved ones you leave behind.

It occurred to me that the *Little Book of Prison* (LDP) would prove useful to you as a first time offender and help you get through what is surely the most difficult time in your life. I wish I had been given the information between these pages, the first weeks would have been better and the learning curve not as steep.

I have dedicated the LBP to my three daughters at the start of the book, but it is also for all my loved ones as well as my fellow prisoners who helped bring together these invaluable guidelines for getting on behind bars. To every reader, good luck with your bird and do yourself a favour and don't go back … Frankie.

2 Getting To Court

2.1 Getting Nicked

Well I'm not sure why you got nicked but it usually has a combination of the following factors:

- money
- drink
- drugs
- women
- cars
- respect
- revenge.

Mine was three of the above: women (separating from my wife); drink (about 30 units a day); and drugs (about five grammes of cocaine a week). I was arrested 25 times in a seven month hyper manic bender, when you're feeling unhappy or in a dark place like I was you just don't think straight. But let me save you from feeling too stupid about how you wound up inside as there is always someone less fortunate than you and a story even more absurd than yours.

Truth is we all do fucked up things and in some cases are worthy of being banged up, sometimes you're just unlucky, sometimes it's for your own good... ultimately even the innocent can go to prison (I hope that's not you by the way). In my case I had been too stupid and suffering from hyper mania for too long. Everyone said if I carried on that way I was going to be either dead, sectioned in a mental institution or in prison.

You are where you are and it is what it is... I think it's safe to say the only one to blame is me, myself and I.

2.2   Police Custody

I learnt a lot from so many arrests and detainments. You will be meeting the following personnel:

- arresting officer
- desk sergeant
- jailers
- cleaners
- solicitors
- interviewing officers
- inspector.

Arresting officers are the front line, I got to know a lot of them in my area and they knew me by name. I was arrested once by six officers in three panda cars, slight overkill if you ask me. Whilst handcuffed and over a bonnet, a BMW (a real police car) pulled up, the window went down and the officer said,

"Evening Mr Owens, will you be doing a fake heart attack with the desk sergeant tonight?"

"Evening Simon you're looking well, I'm not sure yet why."

"Cause if you are we are coming back to the station to watch."

I milked every opportunity to make life difficult for all the personnel except my solicitor … but don't. There's no point giving the jailers grief they will feed you, get you coffee, let you out in the yard for some air and even get you a shower. Always be nice to the jailer.

The food was terrible as it is pre-packed with no sell by date (says it all there, nuclear proof). The breakfast box is a gastronomic crime, it says two succulent pork sausages on the front of the box. I can tell you they ain't fuckin pork and they ain't fuckin succulent!!

Amuse the cleaners as when you can't get the jailer's attention a cleaner can help you to get the jailer. Being angry, shouting threats, banging the door cause you are nicked is no good to no-one especially you.

I am a little claustrophobic so complained of chest pains due to the anxiety which leads to a visit from the ambulance and then a trip to the local A&E. This can burn some time while the arresting officers investigate the alleged crime. You get an escort to the hospital, are handcuffed, put in a wheelchair and flanked by two officers to the A&E department. I am not recommending this of course but I find looking at pretty nurses is better than the four walls of a police cell.

You should only be in for 14 hours or so although my record is 23 (what a beast that was). If you go in drunk don't tell the desk sergeant you are pissed, say you had three pints. If you're a nut bag or behaving nutty calm it down me old son otherwise they will recommend an appropriate adult for the interview. This slows down the process and you'll be in for longer. Ultimately you're a doughnut for getting nicked … I bet if I pushed your nose jam would come out of your ears … if you had a brain you'd be dangerous.

The interview is up to you but if like me you were out of your brain at the time prepare a statement with your solicitor apologising, going guilty and say no comment to everything else. The interview will be quicker and you'll be out sooner. The arresting officer will go off duty and pass on a "case pack" to the next officer on shift. If they can't get further with enquiries they only have 24 hours to hold you. After the interview its back to the cell for the CPS (Crown Prosecution Service) lottery. The case pack is sent to the CPS and they will decide if you are going to court for the arrest or if the desk sergeant will deal with it. I'll give you a clue: you want the desk sergeant.

If it's dragging out to 14 hours plus in the police station then you're unlucky. The cells are terrible, and you're going to meet the inspector who is responsible for all detainees. He or she reviews your case and informs you officially what is happening with your detention. I met the happiest inspector singing and whistling and telling me I was staying in. He even offered me a coffee. I asked why he was so chirpy he replied, "Last day today then I retire!".

2.3 Doctor Blag

I have had hyper mania and been sectioned for six months back when I was younger. It lasted three weeks as the nurses clubbed together and told the chief psychiatrist that I should get out as I was driving everyone NUTS!!

I started to feel this coming back and went to see my doctor years later and took part in trials of medication (meds) to stop me going on uncontrollable benders. It was trial and error really, there are loads of meds they could try you with. I had six or seven different types, all bollocks. My wife brought me a book *The End of My Addiction* and I was introduced to Baclofen a wonder drug that will stop you abusing alcohol or drugs (I had to explain things to the doctor to get to try it).

Most addictions derive from anxiety, a deep-rooted anxiety from some point in your life that makes you take a substance to excess. Baclofen is a muscle relaxant primarily but a secondary effect is that it takes that anxiety away. It works. I went from 30 units a day and five grammes of cocaine to no cravings whatsoever. I was still in a dark place and suffering episodes I fed with drink and cocaine but since being banged up I have not craved a thing. RESULT!

Baclofen will never become a household name for addiction and addicts as the IP (intellectual property) has lapsed so like paracetemol any drug company can make it, so no drug companies can make billions from it like they did with Viagra.

An alcoholic or drug addict can be abstinent for years but still crave the substance everyday. With Baclofen you stop craving completely, you are set free from the binds of self-abuse.

Anyway I would recommend Baclofen if you are going to be banged up. It will definitely help you, Jesus Christ ... you need every bit of help you can get.

However the trouble with Baclofen is that it's not on licence for treating alcohol according to the British Medical Council. HMP X has no doctor, currently rumour is he escaped ... so only relief doctors are available and the head nurse. On review with him to re-prescribe Baclofen he refused based on his fear of being taken to court if I had a medical problem.

"I've been prescribed this from my doctor safely since December."

"You might get appendicitis, we might get taken to court, I will be held responsible (blah blah blah)," he replied.

What a twat!! Baclofen improves your quality of life as an addict but it hasn't been formally recognised by the British Medical Council (because there's no money in it £!). He had all my GP's notes but was too by the book to prescribe it. His defence:

"GPs do funny things."

I assured him this was not an attempt to ruin his fantastic cutting-edge career and that my GP had 20 years experience and was a professional. These people have a duty of care, take a Hippocratic Oath to help people. What a jobsworth. Still I brought in a few weeks' worth to get through the re-adjustment and also applied for Nicorette patches. You will always run out of burn before the next pay day so get some patches to see you through. Funny though, my probation interview, she didn't recommend that I gave up smoking while banged up. The only place where they are promoting smoking, Jesus!

Also try to get a remedial gym pass referral. You can try knee injury, bad back or stress to enable more sessions in the gym and more time out of the cell is a RESULT!!

2.4 Court Appearance

If it's likely you are going to be remanded or convicted (we'll get back to this later). The following are essential:

- money (as much as you've got, £100 ideal)
- fags/tobacco (prison currency)
- new trainers (prison status)
- toothbrush
- skinhead hair cut
- being clean shaven

- names, addresses, telephone numbers and dates of birth.

I was already in a police cell then straight to bang up. I managed another trip to A&E before my Reliance van (see *Chapter 3*) took me to my new home at HMP X. The holding cells at the court are tiny, a third of the size of the larger police cell. I had four hours in there as my case was complicated (gutted, no-good).

Do everything on the form they give you to show how much money you owe out, in my case it was 30K. This should reduce any fines. Also you need legal aid as the cost of a solicitor for me with all the charges and previous court appearances was another few grand.

It makes me laugh the way a solicitor can get a case adjourned because they are not sure they can get paid for their time. I thought the system was about crime and punishment not money in solicitors' pockets.

You need tobacco as it gets you currency to trade for food, toiletries pens, paper ... life's little luxuries. So even if you don't smoke you will need tobacco. New trainers will give you some status with seasoned inmates, Nike Air Max new design or originals, Addidas Gazelle or some classic Nike Cortez. No High Tech as you're more likely to get pushed around the landing, dropped down the queue for a game of pool, or when using the phone or at dinner.

Take your own toothbrush as the HMP standard issue rips your gums to pieces. A skinhead haircut will earn you some status with your fellow inmates and will give you time to find and bribe the wing barber. Be clean shaven as it will look better in court but also gives you a few days banged up before you have to rip your face up with the razor issued by HMP. If you're ever told you're as sharp as a prison razor you're as thick as shit and twice as runny (but you already knew that didn't you?).

As to names, addresses etc., it is a job and a half remembering your own age and date of birth if you were in a similar state to me before I was detained at Her Majesty's pleasure.

If you want to get visits and you have been sentenced (remand visits are easier to arrange than those for convicted prisoners) you need every detail to get your visitors on the list and permission to phone them (phone PIN list). No mobile phone to grab numbers from now Amigo, it's a sheet at induction that makes your mind go blank or blanker depending on your condition.

3 Getting to Prison

3.1 The Reliance Ride

You need to tell them about your claustrophobia otherwise you are in the single compartment vans like you see on the TV when famous criminals are in court. Instead you get the new transit vans which are much nicer, and you can ask them to put some tunes on ("Free Me" by The Who springs to mind but they don't take requests) and the heating. The Reliance workers don't get paid well and don't even know their hours from week to week, a crap job and no mistake. A familiar bit of advice through the LBP is to be friendly, get them talking and crack a few funnies (LBP Rule 1).

I would have tried to get them to go through a Burger King drive through and offered to pay the bill for them as well. This is your last chance to get a meal with real flavour, freshness and heat as once you're banged up the food is shite, shite, shite!! I'm a chef by trade originally and offered to the screw on induction to help in the kitchen.

"No chance, we don't want someone who can cook making the inmates food!"

"Jesus Christ!" as Catherine Tate would have said, "What a load of old shit" (I'll get back to this later).

As you approach HMP you get the feeling of dread and despair and your arse is going 20 pence – 50 pence as it dawns on you that this is your new home. No more sex, drugs and rock 'n roll, time to man up, grin and bear it … as I said before it is what it is and you are where you are.

3.2 First Night

You get unlocked from the Reliance boys and girls and approach the desk. You are asked to sit in a chair — an odd request, it looks like a moulded toilet with a high back. It is a magnetic chair to ensure you are not carrying any concealed weapons, mobile phones, etc. Basic information is taken and then you are put in a holding room.

Be polite, smile at the screws which is again part of LBP Rule 1. If you're not panicking try a joke but make it a short one as your nerves are shot or you're so pissed-off at being banged up. Either way the screws are doing a job so if you try to get them to enjoy it they will be more likely to be helpful. And you need all the help you can get, give them shit if you like but remember shit rolls down.

There are likely to be other prisoners in the holding room so introduce yourself and hope they don't respond with "Bend Over …". If they do, say "Nice to meet you Ben".

Even if it is a seasoned lag the skinhead haircut and new trainers should get you a handshake and the name of your new found friend. Usual topics of conversation are:

"What you in for";

"Where are you from"; or the favourite

"Have you got any burn (tobacco)".

I used the line, "Do you want to see a picture of my sister." Class! I got a smile out of him.

You'll go through to another screw and through some basic paperwork and a chance to order smokers packs and phone credits. If you have money, as advised, then get two things sorted, tobacco and phone credits. I had 1p in my pocket so was given an emergency £5 which after a smokers pack, Amber Leaf, Rizla and your official HMP prison lighter (keep this they are worth a few quid on eBay when you get out) I had £1.40 for phone credit. By the time I'd rung my wife and spoken to my eldest daughter there was nothing left.

I didn't know it would take two weeks to get more credit on the card. Fuck! (I told my little girl daddy was away working!).

You will then meet the insider, an inmate who gives you your kit, wonderful clothes, bedding, toiletries and a breakfast pack. Again use LBP Rule 1 and ask for an extra blanket as the cells are freezing at night. Tell them you have athlete's foot, foot root, trench foot (means your feet stink) and you might get extra socks. But bear in mind they've heard it all before.

Next comes my personal favourite, the strip search … get ready to touch your toes pretty eyes its Friday night again already!!! Pray for a screw with thin fingers. No time for a post penetration burn you dress in the grey tracksuit come pyjamas, burgundy T-shirt, your new trainers and grey socks. Congratulations you have your "Ticket to Torment". You are now a part of the tribe you doughnut.

If you want your own cell you have to say you are racist, claustrophobic and a self-abuser. Dave, a new inmate, has a cell with major damp in it and a smackhead for a cell mate who shits ten times a day … what a beast he is having!!! Rule 2 of LBP: "There's always someone worse off than you sweet pea". Thinking about it I wish my wife was as dirty as Dave's cell.

You're then through to the holding area while they process which wing and which cell you will be in. It's the prison lottery, but like Dave there are losers as well as winners. I tried the self-abuser approach saying I was a sex addict and had to knock one out seven times a day. They didn't go for it.

My first cell mate is a first offender who although 15 years my junior is a sound guy who is friendly, a laugh, clean and tidy and shares his stuff with you. I was a cell mate lottery winner, it's what I would call a "Wight Touch".

You also get to make a phone call from the £5 credit they give you when you first arrive, less your smokers pack leaves £1.40. Don't ring a mobile ever!! Use a landline number, mobiles fly through your credit. You need to make the call brief as you won't get any more credit on the phone for at least a week. In my case it was nearly two weeks, another lottery is which day you got in — Tuesday is the worst (guess what day I came in … Yep, last thing Monday evening, so fuckin' Tuesday was my first day).

You also get your first taste of prison food. People will say as did I that the food is shite … well it is, but like hospital food it is definitely edible. There is a limited choice, it is overcooked and lukewarm but that's on the wing. This first meal lulls you into a false sense of security, it's hot out of the microwave and it's OK, unlike that on the wing. There were three seasoned inmates in the second holding area so me being me and applying LBP Rule 1 I started talking to them. They were on their way to a D-Cat prison where there would be lots of liberty minimum lock up (lucky bastards, I'm in a B-Cat here). They told me they came in from HMP Brixton and that my new home was the worst prison in the country. I shrugged it off as per LBP Rule 3, in short:

"Don't believe anything or anyone".

I chatted for a bit to the Afro-Caribbean guy with the gold tooth who looked like the top boy of the three. He reckoned I was blagging him.

"You done bird before?"

"Not me mate, it's the first time and the last time."

"Na, bruv you bin in before."

I just grinned and said, "Not me fella I'm just misunderstood."

This is very true. My hyper manic break started back in April 2010 and ran to January 2011 but I'm not angry about my detainment. I knew something had to stop my destructive behaviour. As I'm writing this I have just received a note from my Dad. I've been in for six days so far. It reads:

Hi Frankie

Hope you are OK keep your chin up, won't be long, behave yourself, we want the real Frankie back,

Lots of Love Dad xxx (enclosed £40 postal order).

I'm named after my dad and his dad so I'm Frankie Owens Jnr the 3rd. I'm very proud of my name and my family but since April 2010 (and probably before that) I have treated them badly and been a very selfish bastard.

As he said the real Frankie wouldn't have got 25 arrests and nine convictions in his right mind but on a hyper manic bender it was chaos theory. I have a degree, a masters degree, a great house a senior management career, a wife and three children. They say that a gentleman knows where the line is drawn and never crosses it. I knew where the line was drawn and constantly crossed it.

I'm not sure any loved one is proud of me at the moment. I'm not proud of me either. But as I said earlier when you are unhappy or in a dark place you just can't think straight. When you add the amount of alcohol and coke I was using it made me detach not just from reality but from my core values, or as my dad put it from the real Frankie. How the fuck do you know what you're going to do until you do it!! The answer is you don't and hindsight is a wonderful thing (no shit).

Anyway, back to the chapter. You are then told to grab your stuff and go to your new home. The cell is 14 feet by 8 feet. I'm slightly claustrophobic which does not help in bang up, the cell is so small and when I turn the light off I'm already in bed before it goes dark. Cell standard furniture: two beds, a toilet, a sink, some rickety table, a locker, a kettle and the one thing that will save your life and sanity, a television. RESULT!

Without the TV you would definitely go mad/crack up/climb the walls. You settle in, make a cup of tea with your plastic spoon in your plastic cup, chat to your new cell mate, make the bed, all that bullshit, then the TV goes off and you hear the seasoned inmates banging doors, you hear keys jangling, shouting and screaming and you wish to fuck you were anywhere but here. If you end up with tears rolling down your cheeks its OK, if you've got boy glue rolling down your other cheeks then its game over … goodnight Gord Bless Ya.

3.3 Cell Etiquette

Day Seven of my first bang up and the first signs of violence on the wing were on view today. I'm pretty sure in prison bingo that is a full house!! It was the only missing experience to behold. Lots of speculation on why it happened and who did what but as LBP Rule 3 says, "Don't believe anyone".

All I can say is it changes the mood of association. I would have guessed it was LBP Rule 4 ("Pay your bills if you borrow") but who knows. One of the inmates is now off the wing (I got a big mug off the fella on day two, he knows some of the Pompey faces I know, by association of course!). I also met the first face from my chaos period. He has been in three times already, 20-years-old a little glue sniffer who, fair to say, is a doughnut (push his nose and jam definitely comes out of his ears).

Your cell is tiny and you're co-habiting with your new celly. Eighty per cent of all prisoners take drugs, so clean the cell the moment you get in. In 2011 there were 85,000 prisoners in the UK, 68,000 drug users, talk about a captive market. Boil the kettle and sanitise the taps, the sink and the toilet with boiling water. Hepatitis B is rife inside and you are offered the Hep B jab at induction. You must take it me old mate, take it all day long. You don't want your legacy of prison to be contracting Hep B.

33

If you're a prison lottery loser and your cell mate is a little smack rat don't go twos on his burn. Don't walk bare feet in the cell. We had used razor blades on the floor and you don't know who was in your cell last. Stick your UHT milk on the window sill overnight. UHT milk is shite, at least cold it's less shite. Also put your socks out of the window to air overnight, socks are like innocent inmates in prison … hard to find.

Toothpaste makes excellent Blue-Tac substitute with all my lovely ladies on the wall smelling of fluoride. Me being me I have added speech bubbles stuck to their mouths with phrases like:

"You're my daddy Frankie"; and

"Frankie you're so big, do it again".

Blow your nose and clear your throat before bed and ask your pad mate to do the same as this will minimise the snoring. On that note try to get to sleep first, a hard skill to master but you don't get your cell mate snoring as your last noise before you nod off.

Take regular showers, sounds obvious, but a definite once you get over the stereotype of getting jumped. My first shower was two minutes panicking like a bastard and I'm old, ugly and out of shape. Another prison lottery is the fun game of chasing the hot water.

This runs alongside finding the best block and the best cubicle if you have them. Some inmates will shower with their boxers on or use the shower to wash their clothes, not my bag but please yourself. Showers when you get all the above right are a welcome treat even though you are stuck with prison issue shampoo and soap. The prison issue Shave Gel makes a fair hair gel if you just want to give it a little texture. Don't worry for now, a few weeks in and you can get some real toiletries from the canteen (more later).

Cell fishing or "running a line" allows you to pass items to the cells directly below you. You'll need to rip the sides off of the bedding sheet and tie these together and use your plastic bags from your breakfast packs. Careful though because if you're not a pro at fishing you may lose your items for good.

Share with your celly and he will share with you, you will get further as a double act than on your own, again it's a lottery as they might tuck you up, but you need to work together so give it a shot. If he lets you down it will be too late. He would have already been shipped out.

You'll also learn a lot from seasoned inmates. A great quote from one of them:

"Boys mature into men and more knowledgeable crooks" (Jason Smith, HMP Birmingham).

Kleptomania is rife in your new home, one of my new inmates Dave (with the crap cell and smack head celly) came back from taking a shower at association to find someone had nicked his TV. When you leave your cell always make sure it is locked up even if you're only going to be two seconds. If you have a celly then they can keep an eye on it but if not make sure it's locked.

On the last day before canteen your fellow inmates are climbing the walls and will go on the hunt for anything worth trading. One of the fellas on our floor had his last bit of burn nicked and as he grabbed the thief he said, "Your gonna hear three hits, me hitting you, you hitting the floor and the ambulance hitting 90 miles an hour".

Don't whatever you do write your name on the cell wall. It is bad luck, the old inmates who have worn a sentence or two will say, "If you write your name on the wall you'll be back one day to wipe it off".

Don't get angry the cell has no room for emotions — in fact it has got no room for anything much.

Sink plugs are harder to come by than a fillet steak at dinner but no worries. Squash tissue paper into the shape of the plug hole and use your breakfast pack plastic to cover it and turn the ends clockwise until tight and knot the end. Voilà, a prison cell plug.

I've just had my canteen sheet through the cell door and it says "0.34 pence". Mate it's like all my Christmases have come early. I had money sent in but this has not appeared on the sheet so no decent toiletries for me for a few weeks (I smell like a hospital ward). My first item is a pencil sharpener and pencil to continue to write the LBP. I am also forced to tick burn at double bubble what an interest rate that is!!! It's criminal!

Taking a dump, dropping the kids off at the pool, this needs to be humane to your cell mate. Choose association and leave the windows and doors open to air the room. On a few occasions I have had a screw peer into the cell and catch me in the turd act

"Can't you see I'm busy … I can't take this shit anymore."

I heard a story that a new inmate came into a seasoned lag's cell and for a giggle during the night the seasoned lag moved the beds together. The joke backfired, the young lad went ballistic and ended up on the punishment block. I wouldn't recommend pushing the beds together.

Getting Through Induction

4.1 Probation

If you managed to sleep on your first night, nice work, you can't get any luckier, and your living the dream. It's going to get better, you are all set for Induction Phase 2.

You're taken from the main wing to a portakabin/classroom. You get your first view of your fellow inmates as around eight-ish 'til nine-ish in this prison is Golden Hour. I can't think of anything golden about it. Nada, nil, zilch. It may be called "golden" but it's never an hour. FACT.

I'm seeing loads of skinheads, trainers connected to half asleep fellas walking the landing with buckets of rubbish asking each other for a burn, Rizla or yesterday's papers. A week into my first and last visit to prison and I can't remember how I felt being in the first Golden Hour, it seems a long time ago. You get to use the phone, go on exercise, hand in forms — but I will come back to that later.

Take your seat in the classroom and get ready for the first section of Induction Phase 2 ... Probation DVD and presentation. However someone had nicked the TV, no lie it had disappeared … the prison issue tracksuit doesn't even have pockets.

Thinking about how comfortable I have felt banged up and how other inmates have treated me probably has a little to do with the amount of programmes and films I've watched about prison. Films I would recommend watching are "McVicar", a classic with Roger Daltrey lead singer of The Who. The soundtrack is different class — the film starts with the track "FREE ME", another track goes "DON'T PLEAD NO SPECIAL CASE FOR ME … CAUSE THERE AINT NO WAY I'LL GET MY LIBERTY". It's the story of John McVicar who got 12 years for armed robbery and ended up doing a PhD. If I stay in I'll do my PhD as it costs 15K on the outside.

Another classic is "Scum" with a very young Ray Winston, it's about borstal. There's a character in the film called Archer. He is a hero of mine. Archer is anti-establishment, highly intelligent and likes to bend people's heads … he's different gravy. But the crème de la crème is the comedy series "Porridge" with Ronnie Barker and Richard Beckinsale. That show will knock you on your arse, it's hilarious and gives you the right mentality for prison. Godber (Beckinsale) is a first timer and Fletch (Barker) is the older, seasoned jail bird. Fletch teaches Godber to "bide his time", "keep your chin up" and states, "If you can't do the time, don't do the crime". Like "Only Fools and Horses" I can watch this again and again, it is class.

So if the TV isn't nicked you still get the probation officer to have a chat with you. I had an excellent pre-sentence report (PSR) for the first six crimes I was up for. In the magistrates' court they will be swayed by your PSR and its recommendations. I was cautioned for two crimes and NFA (no further action) on another two ... it could have been much worse. It was the other two more serious offences committed whilst on bail that got me remanded at Her Majesty's pleasure. You will get a one to one interview with probation if you're on remand which might get you bail but all in good time as all processes inside take a long time (three weeks plus). Wait till you hear about the time frame on canteen sheets later, they are no-good to no-one. The trouble for me with the bail issue was I was back in court on the 25th of February so if bail had been possible the report would not have been processed in time anyway as induction was the 2nd of February.

Prison is full of lottery games as bang up is so long there are not enough minutes in association or golden time to get everything done. This morning the queue for meds, my beloved Baclofen was "bear long". It's a saying I've learnt from my celly D-Cat Dave, a nickname I have given him since he has been re-classified and scheduled for an open prison. RESULT! But the prison involved has been half burnt down by inmates who got twatted on New Year's Eve and set fire to a block. Those inmates had maximum liberty and still burnt it down (wankers). Chances are I'll be out before D-Cat Dave gets processed to the open prison. Anyway I wanted to go out to the exercise yard, pick up meds and get an application form. I just managed the meds and the yard. This is why you need your celly to help, he got the application form and much needed crap toiletries and crap paper … for crapping … other crap paper is provided for letters by the cleaner orderly.

4.2   CARAT

Probation over a quick cup of prison tea and a burn, it's now time for CARAT. Not a ginger joke or a root vegetable it stands for Counselling, Assessment, Referral, Advice and Throughcare (Why do people call ginger haired people carrot tops … carrot tops are green?). Viv was the lady heading CARAT, a brunette before you ask. She said she hadn't seen any of our faces before … I couldn't resist, me being me …

"We have met Viv."

"Have we?"

"Yes you were drunk at the nightclub and I lent you a score (£20). I'm just here to pick up the 20 quid."

The class cracked up, Viv cracked up and went a cherry red, the screw cracked up and so did the insiders. I have always been the same, a classroom was my favourite place to entertain at 36 years ten months and I am still a juvenile delinquent, it's why I get on so well with kids, I have the same mental age.

I will sit next to my daughter at Sunday dinner round the in-laws and put mash or sauce on my face, turn to her and say, "Have I got any food on my face". I'll make the tea and bring in empty mugs and pretend to trip and spill them over the nan in law or mother in law (the Witches of Eastwick: lovely people, really, honest!). The family have seen this stunt many times, my wife rolls her eyes and I giggle to myself. I've been doing this since I was a 14-year-old waiter. It's still funny in Frankie Land a wicked place to visit but you wouldn't want to live there!

CARAT is a worthy cause and will get you out of your cell so sign up to everything they offer and express your addictions to drink drugs and general excess. It will do you a favour, you can't lose on this one. If you are doing too much it will help you learn tools and thought exercises to curtail your enthusiasm. If you don't you will hear stories from inmates in your group meetings that will help, give you a reason not to let drink and drugs take you over. Also you are out of the cell, your constant mission in HMP X. I'm going to go for the acupuncture as I have never had it before. I didn't fancy it then and it just goes to show how when in HMP the thought of having needles stuck into you is suddenly appealing... Jesus.

I had a key worker on the out, a counsellor, and went to Alcoholics Anonymous (AA) meetings, which I had reservations about. Some of these people were at the very bottom of their cages at the time I was on the way down but had not hit the bottom... that's prison for me.

Ultimately the only one that can help you is you. The tools CARAT can provide will help you to focus and reflect on your consumption and behaviour under the influence. It's up to you of course but I can tell you that the humiliation of prison is teaching me humility... sometimes.

I have had the chance to read since being inside and taking Baclofen, it's the combination of no anxiety and having time on my hands that has allowed me to keep still and read. The first book I have read and finished since being inside is *The Man that Sold the Eiffel Tower* a book about a con man in the 19th century (he sold it twice for scrap metal). A great book is *Catcher in the Rye* by J D Salinger. He is a bit of me. There is a quote in it when his professor gives him some advice, he's been expelled from a private school, he writes the quote on a piece of paper, J D is heading for a fall — the same as being in HMP X you never find out how he falls — but the advice says:

> The mark of an immature man is that he wants to die nobly for a cause, while the mark of the mature man is that he wants to live humbly for one.

It's a bit heavy I know and with my immature brain I'm not sure I will take notice of it completely, but I'm sure had I been humble and had humility I would not be in HMP X.

You're always going to be riding a fall of some kind if you're out of control, trouble is being out of control can be exciting, an addiction in itself — as long as you grow older learning from your mistakes and don't keep making the same mistakes over and over.

Ah well being is prison is permanent ... for now ...

4.3 The Chaplaincy

Gord Bless Ya ... Its Day Eleven at HMP x and I was told my snoring and talking in my sleep was keeping D-Cat Dave up for a while last night (I forgot to blow my nose and clear my throat poor bastard).

I spoke to my little girl this morning, she is hilarious, six-year-olds say the funniest things. She explained that her chill blade on her foot had come from nowhere. She also made me sad as she is supposed to be writing a diary and she said she is drawing sad faces. One of the worst things about detainment is not seeing my little girl and gorgeous twin girls and the love of my life the wife, her indoors, the enemy. Even though we have been separated for nine months I still love her, she's the most beautiful woman I have ever met but we have been like reverse magnets, bringing out the worst in each other (also down to my hyper manic consumption rates).

I had an induction for education yesterday and had to do a basic numeracy and literacy test. Going through the maths questions took me back to my schooldays and reminded me of my wife in her school uniform. She looked mean and moody at school, same as today in fact, we were childhood sweethearts.

A lady called Judith did an interview with me at the education induction about my options, I can't do the PhD unless I have a sentence of six months or longer. Judith has had 20 years of counselling alcoholics (just my luck) and so we quickly got talking about my detainment at HMP X and the major part my consumption had played in it. She asked if I would stop taking alcohol and drugs when I got out. Once again I got defensive as I tend to do. To D-Cat Dave or family I am clear that the drink and drugs are over, no more, finished, but to Judith I had to contextualise the issue, throw in comparisons, quote famous drinkers, my favourite is Winston Churchill:

"I took more out of drink than drink took out of me".

I am definitely a non-conformist with a mischievous streak. The Monday to Friday, nice house 2.4 children, wash the car on Sunday, rat race, chasing the money, go on a better holiday, keep up with the Jones's life, I called mundanium. There has to be more to life than this... then again HMP X is no life at all in comparison.

There's no question that HMP X has halted the destructive pattern of my life in the last ten months. It's one of those things to tick off the list: "Been to prison". The silver lining of my time at HMP X is that I'm fitter, I've lost weight, I'm getting lots of rest, I'm off the drink and drugs and I'm working on *The Little Book of Prison*. Also I needed to brush up on my Excel skills, I've signed up for the European Computer Driving Licence. I used to sell these when I was a senior manager at a university that ran short courses, I also went to Milton Keynes Cat-A prison to sell qualifications to the Prison Service a year ago. I never imagined that a year later I would be a customer of a prison studying for a qualification... Jesus I'm seeing the education system from every angle.

I should be seeing my counsellor today for my last session of 12 if I was on the outside, I am sure she would be shaking her head but ultimately would not be surprised by my bang up ... sorry Ru you tried your best.

Well the chaplain's talk was brief ... apologies for the rant, I was definitely on one there ... religion is not my bag. My mum is C of E and my dad is Catholic. I have never been christened and not been a choirboy or gone to church. I did sing "Walking in the Air" Alled Jones-style to my junior school once before my balls dropped but that was about it.

The chaplaincy will get you out of the cell on a Wednesday night for a social session and on Sunday of course. I am not sure you could convince the chaplin that you were "multiple faith" as this would give you three hours on Sunday, Catholic and C of E, and midweek prayer as a Muslim, plus all the socials ... give it a try and let me know how you get on. Also if you're a Muslim you will get your canteen a day early as you are in prayer Friday afternoon.

I'm reading a book called *Alcohol: Thriller or Killer* in which the inmate finally finds religion as a born again Christian. God spoke to him and stopped his craving for alcohol. Interesting that he doesn't classify alcoholism as a disease even though it had gripped him for 30 years, he reckons it's a SIN. I find it difficult to agree based on my background in hospitality and experience of celebrations, events and networking with alcohol and people. On the other hand if there had been no booze then there would be no bird ... food for thought ... to be continued. The best thing about the chaplaincy talk is getting a diary to put your telephone numbers, notes, to-do lists in — ready for the Golden Hour runaround.

D-Cat Dave has just been told he's off to open prison tomorrow. I ticked some burn and split it with Dave as he may be gone before his canteen arrives so I'll be stuck with his debt (bollocks). The other Dave is going to move in tomorrow (better the fellow you know), he's 26 another first offender and in for forgery and fraud, he'll be alright.

The local newspaper has just reported on the front page about a lady chaplain who worked at HMP X. She had problems with drink 15 years previously, had found God and was now a trusted visitor to the prison. She was found in a "compromising position" the paper said ... I've never done that one, but I put my back out trying the wheelbarrow once in Tenerife. She was sentenced to 18 months for bringing vodka, mobile phones and energy bars into the prison. Was it the demon drink that pulled her in or the falling in love with an inmate, or if the mobile was an i4 with all the extras maybe that's what she was after ... they say God moves in mysterious ways — but probably not the wheelbarrow.

4.4 The Gym

The most tiring job in bang up is doing nothing... serious... either that or there's something in the water.

The one thing I said I would sort out if I got into HMP was to get fit... easy idea as you don't have anything to do and it gets you out of your cell and gives you extra association time. Trouble is the list you have to sign up for comes out in the evening the day before gym and I'm on the 3rd floor with 180 inmates on my wing. By the time we get let out the list is full and I'm on the reserve list (what a beast!). If you work or do the CARAT courses (see *Chapter* 4.2) they will automatically put you on the gym list, another reason to do the CARAT course. If you do education courses the same will apply.

You get two gym sessions a week unless you have pulled off the doctor blag and got a remedial note, then its every day. My times are Monday and Wednesday mornings. Now forgive me, but would it not be easier to have these a bit further apart to allow my body to recover. It took me until day 21 to get on the list and on day 22 I am aching all over. Tomorrow will be worse as that's my next gym session!! I'm also doing press ups, curls and shoulder raises in the cell using the metal bed frame. Start slow and build yourself up. Charles Bronson (one of the most notorious prisoners in the UK) is said to do 1,000 press ups a day... good luck with that. HMP time is all about punishment so you might as well put your body through it as well, ready — one, two, three ... LIFT! At my age, 36 years new, looking 25, the better the shape I can be in the more likely I am to get younger girls ... or older girls ... or any girls on the outside. Maybe my wife would have me back ... maybe I would have my wife back ... women are funny fellas, maybe I'll become a monk but without the God bit.

I got on the reserve list for the gym and managed to get into the gym itself. We were led through a small door where a hatch dispenses a pair of dark blue shorts and a light blue ... VEST. I've never, never worn a vest since I moved to a new school and the first day in was PE. I had to wear the flea bag lost property massive shorts, vest and plimsolls, two sizes too big for me. Of course this led to the boys giving me loads of stick on the rugby pitch so I had my habitual fight on the first day with the biggest of the group a guy called Mark. I didn't win of course as I'm a pacifist, a lover not a fighter, more mental abuse not physical abuse. I've never seen the pleasure of putting fists and kicks into another person. But I appreciate that standing your ground is important and back then it was worth a few digs. He's now a cage fighter. I called him a few months ago and offered him out (a mutual friend had given me his number). He answered the phone:

"Who this?"

"I'm gonna do you you big mug its payback time."

"Anytime, anywhere, who is this?"

"Its Frankie Owens ... How are you fella?"

"Fuck me, Frankie how are ya?"

Anyway, I've never seen anything like a prison gym session. Somewhere the size of a squash court packed with weights, machines and 40 inmates, all huge! I was lucky there were three or four inmates the same size as me, so I was not the last turkey in the shop, just the third last!!

It's similar to Wacky Races in the gym, these boys were training fast and hard, I got through nine machines, three sets on each and a ten minute run before it was all over. I recommend the gym but would steer clear of the bench press. Showing you are in a certain strength division in HMP X is easy by your size but showing that you can't lift a bar with two crisp packets attached I would not advise, but that's just me I guess.

All inmates will respect the fact that you want to train and they all started somewhere so it's a must for you, you little rat. I remember asking a bodybuilder in a pub where the toilets were. He pushed his arms together in a tense pose and pointed saying, behind gritted teeth, "Its over there."

The steroid business is booming among the gym heads and you can see the difference in training capability and the mood swings on the landing, could be why a lot of them wear boxers in the shower... twig and berries syndrome!! A muscle they can't work... Viagra doesn't sell in here at all, surprise, surprise, surprise.

4.5 Money

I blagged my way into a VIP area at the Goodwood Festival of Speed, where a drunken, toffee-nosed chap, all Harris Tweed, informed me, "Money is just a bur...den dear fellow". He was holding a large bottle of champagne and hiccupping at the time. I said, "Allow me to unburden you sir, lend me a bulls-eye" (£50).

Money is as critical in prison as it is anywhere in any situation but even more so in prison. It's called canteen, you get a canteen sheet to put your choices on, but this form only comes on a Monday and if you came in with no money like me then there's nothing on it. I came in on the Monday evening so it took a full week to receive a canteen sheet and using the phone credit before you are told how to get money in is backwards and bent. So save some money on the phone credit, but because your reading the LBP you brought money in with you so the canteen sheet has money on it.

You get an opportunity to get a smokers pack while on induction on day two — ask for the maximum number of these packs, three. This will get to you on the second Friday of your bird. Try getting half an ounce of tobacco to last eleven days … impossible when every inmate is asking you for a burn and your stress is at its highest. On the out I was smoking 30 to 40 fags a day so had to go down the road of ticking tobacco at double bubble 100 per cent interest. The going rate is 50 per cent but as a new fish (as they say in the USA) you will be stung for double bubble all day long. The boredom makes you smoke more for sure (and the stress of the walls closing in). Money sent in needs to be a postal order to HM Prison Service with your name and prisoner number on. Get them to put it on the envelope and on a Post-it note and put that on the postal order itself … are you with me?

We arrived on Monday 1st February in the evening so on Friday 11th my wish list smokers packs arrived, ordered on induction on the 2nd Feb. As mentioned earlier in this LBP, on Monday 14th Feb my first canteen sheet had next to nothing left from my emergency £5. I ordered a pencil sharpener to help write LBP. I'd been slicing my fingers on prison razor blades trying to sharpen a pencil (my thumb looked like a serious self-harmer). On Monday 21st my canteen sheet arrived with some money on sent in by my dad, so finally I could order something meaningful. The sharpener arrived on Friday 25th Feb ... I think you can see the nightmare of the first few weeks.

The first letter you send out, ask for stamps and envelopes. You can use these to trade for tobacco, then if you don't smoke, buy some luxuries. It will take months to work up to the lending of a DVD player or Play Station 2. I managed to get my hands on a DVD player in week four. RESULT!

Day 12. Today and yesterday were low days, talking to my daughter and wife played on my mind all day and in prison it kills you. I had to reinforce LBP Rule 1. Time is more than bearable if you shut down your emotions, block out your feelings, unfortunately using this skill can turn you cold hearted. Some inmates finish with partners before they go in as this is the only way that they can handle their bird (forgive the pun). A good con man can replicate any emotion but feels none. My bender behaviour gave me Jekyll and Hyde personalities — Hyde would block out and shut down emotions, Jekyll is the real Frankie. Since being in HMP the trick is to be Jekyll but shield emotions (a difficult but necessary task at HMP). It's letters today so I will be writing to my wife and my brother again and this will stir up feelings.

Some of the seasoned inmates are playing the Hyde card so hard as it is the only way they will make it through prison. Some are Hyde all the time, that's why they are in HMP in the first place. It's up to you mate to do what you gotta do. Either way you need to get out in one piece so just ride your bang up.

If you're thinking of coming back to prison you may be aspiring to be a PPO (persistent prolific offender). Don't worry about emptying your canteen account it will still be here when you get back in. Your prisoner number will also be the same along with your telephone PIN and numbers list. I remember thinking there might be an HMP card for your account and a hole in the wall, and I laughed and laughed and laughed but that's only in Frankie Land of course. A hole in the wall in prison ... that will be the day.

Getting Through First Weeks

5.1 Boredom

In my new home you're locked up 22 hours a day. By that painful restriction the four walls are a boring prospect, make no mistake. Thank God you have a telly (and ordered *TV Choice* from the library, 42p well spent). Prisoners used to count bricks in the cell (not recommended), "Death by Eastenders" is a killer, although "Emmerdale" is a must. I'd love to visit a small country village with as many young fit ladies in it.

We have three pool tables and two sets of pool balls (figure that one out) and a table tennis table on our wing. It will take you a while to get into the pecking order to get a game of pool. I have yet to see the table tennis bats and ball 12 days into my bird although I did hear someone playing during their association (the wing is three floors and association is by floor, one morning, one afternoon, one in the evening, 60 inmates each). I'm gutted as I used to play exhibition table tennis with my little brother on the holiday camps. He was tiny at the time and it looked great smashing the ball at a tiny lad in a tracksuit too big for him. We used to play with tiny bats, frying pans all sorts of props, easy money, betting a punter £5 on a game with a miniature bat, ching ching!

Association for standard prisoners with no work or education is one hour per day so don't hold your breath about opening the doors late — and getting you behind your door early happens frequently, but at least you can watch some pool. Exercise is a welcome change. You get to walk round in a concrete yard the size of two tennis courts. Like a demented hamster or a lab rat going round and round anti-clockwise (don't ask why anti-clockwise, no idea, seems like we were going backwards in time) and it's hilarious to think that this relieves the boredom, but I'm telling you it does.

According to the Induction Manual there are board games available on the wing. I haven't seen any. I asked a screw who told me they were all out never to be seen again. In HMP X even Monopoly would be highly entertaining (that's saying something). I did once spot some dominos but when I asked if I could borrow them they told me they were theirs. Being Day Three I wasn't going to argue.

The library is tiny but is the place to save your mind from your new home. It sounds cheesy but books inside HMP X can set you free, pure escapism from your four walls. I'm getting access to the library one day a week and you have to pester the screws to make sure they let you have access. You can order books but they will take a while to get through. I had a list of books I had wanted to read for years. I only found one of them after the first two visits, but I got through it in three days, it was brilliant (laughed out loud, funny in parts).

Writing is my gig hence the LBP but finding paper and pens is difficult before your canteen kicks in. In your case it's two weeks as you have LBP to guide you, so use your letters to ask for paper, envelopes and stamps, etc. My new cell mate, Dave Two likes art and is drawing a few bits — any opportunity for creative expression I would recommend.

Visits will break up the day if you can handle them (or if any one loves you). My Dad has just sent me a letter, funny as my mum sent me one yesterday. I swear you can't help but read them over and over. I'm not sure if it's the boredom or the connection with my loved ones that compels me to read but there is a definite comfort to it. You need to send visitor forms with your letters and will need the date of birth for each of them. This gets your brain going, remembering exactly how old your parents are and your wife's or girlfriend's birthday, you're in enough trouble as it is so don't get the birthday wrong.

If you're on remand your visitors can just telephone in and arrange a visit but remember they need to have a photo ID. At HMP X the visitor facility is a new build and not too prison-like, 34 tables with a red chair for the inmate and three blue chairs on the other side of the moulded table and chair combo. It's like the tables at a swimming pool viewing area except these are screwed to the floor and you're watched by CCTV and eight screws. Considering how short staffed HMP X always seems to be there are plenty of screws in the visits area.

You're grabbed from your cell and penned into the holding areas. Through new doors and up and down steps it's the prison Donkey Derby with all the runners half asleep from their afternoon kip. Into the last pen before the visits room and there are two black bins with green vests or red vests, Green BO stench ones for remand prisoners and red even stinkier tramp vests for the sentenced. I was down on the list as a convicted criminal so I asked, "Really, how long did I get. I'm not due in court till the 25th". The screw replied, "Not sure but convicted prisoners get longer visit time than remand so keep quiet". Another prison lottery win for me.

One of the inmates had kept us waiting while he freshened up for his missus, not sure it was worth the precious Lynx deodorant stick (£2.69 off the canteen sheet) as the vests are so rank. I reckon they could walk in all by themselves. My table was No. 22. I sat on my red criminal's chair and watched as the first wave of loved ones came in. Watching the hugging, kissing, smiling and tears as they sat around their screwed down tables was a rare glimpse of civilisation, a little piece of normal life in the HMP X limbo.

My dad arrived ten minutes after I had sat down and started watching the other prisoners' visits and listening to the conversations. He had been searched and sniffed out by a drug sniffer dog, what a joy for him. We got a good hour together and it was great to see him. Your visitor can bring change in and treat you to coffee, two cups, for me it was excellent ... well rubbish vending machine crap but when you have only had prison tea for weeks and only two coffees it was the finest choice crap. Chocolate bars are also available, the best Kit Kat dark (I hate dark chocolate on the outside) and Mars Bars (superb). The simple pleasures on the out are so savoured when banged up.

The visitors are not allowed to pass anything across and prisoners are not allowed to put their hand to their mouth. This is to prevent smuggling ... yeah, right, 34 inmates against eight screws and the CCTV whilst they are eating and drinking, you can guess the odds can't you. The screw calls time at the tables ... "Lads and lasses lets have your glasses (empty paper cups in this case)". Then the final hugs and kisses and tears and squeezing of arses and it's all over, back to the Donkey Derby and chez cell.

Your cell mate also gets the bonus of some personal time, Dave Two looked very very relaxed when I got back!!

Decorating your cell will give you some purpose, you need to employ LBP Rule 1 and get around the landing and cells and ask for newspapers. You may have ordered *Nuts* or *Zoo* with your first canteen as you had money cause you had read LBP *Chapters 1* and *2*. No need for the *Financial Times*, not that you would find one in HMP X. You do need the *Sun* and the *Star* where your new cell decoration is found on page three, or the *Sunday Sport*, in which case every page has potential. These newspapers make excellent wallpaper, for artistic appreciation of course! Although the minute my collection was growing one of the lady screws came into the cell and told me that naked women were now banned from being on the walls!! Unbelievable, one of the few pleasures available to you at HMP X and it has been made a reportable offence (They will never get me to bend to this one, nor you I suspect).

Chatting to the lady screws is also a pastime but again you only get the chance in association, depending on the to do list for the day and the prison lottery of who you have on your wing to choose from against the criteria of your type (there's a mouthful but you have to cram it all into the Golden Hour). Let me tell you, as time progresses your tastes may change significantly and that's without the beer goggles.

Making tea is another ritual in the cell which you will be repeating six times a day at least. I have been in for 260 cups of tea and four coffees, and I will have another 1,400 cups to serve before I'm released. Tea-making goes hand in hand with rolling and smoking the thinnest roll-ups you have ever seen, three drags and they're out. On Saturdays we are given a pack of biscuits, Happy Shopper own label-type of course but I have to say I've never enjoyed dipping bikkies in tea as much in my life. Peter Kay the comedian did a sketch about bikkies dropping into his tea, no chance in here — dip and munch in the blink of an eye. Simple pleasures that are the highlight of the week before your canteen arrives … it's only in six days' time … it will fly by!

Afternoon naps can relieve your boredom state but beware you'll be awake half the night unless you're planning on hibernating your bird away, and you'll then miss the Golden Hour which means nothing will get done (Unless your cell mate is running errands for you).

Personal time (PT) is aka self-abuse … you know knocking one out … spanking the monkey … flogging the dolphin might be your thing but this is a tricky one if you don't have a single cell. You can tell inmates who have a single cell as they have no colour in their face and walk around like John Wayne … they would give their left arm (not right of course) for an ice pack for their balls. Hope your cell mate is joining education or work or a CARAT course, the chances in the first few weeks is unlikely but their visits of course will be possible PT moments for you. Even when you have the place to yourself you are still chancing getting caught. D-Cat Dave got caught out when I went to be tested for education, pants well and truly down, beads of sweat running down his forehead, very red faced as one of the inmates opened the door flap looking for a Rizla.

Cards – I've managed to get a pack of cards 12 days into my bang up. RESULT!! But Dave Two can't play cards so its clock patience for me, not the result I thought it would be. The cards were on their last legs, torn and smelling of prison, had passed through hundreds of sweaty criminal hands. The cards were advertising the dangers of Hep B … more like they were carriers … they did not look well.

Memories – I'm also a fan of good memories to relieve the boredom. I've always been brought up in sociable surroundings, my dad ran holiday camps which meant I was around a lot of people all of the time which was a great upbringing. My favourite weekend was coming home from school to 350 majorettes, you know girls in short skirts, sparkly costumes, twirling batons. I thought all my Christmases and birthdays had come at once, 12-years-old and in a Rick Ashley 1980s suit and deck shoes. I became a professional baton twirler of sorts that weekend. Try to stay away from the bad ones, the classic mistake is to recall the recent memories of why you are in HMP X … no good to no-one especially you as a first timer.

Trading with other prisoners will give you hours of boredom relief. If you can get to the long-term prisoners they have radios, DVD players, and Play Station 2s, the most wanted asset in prison (for prisoners and screws on the night shift). The more you get around the wing the more chance you have of getting more traders, finding tea bags, whitener and sugar, food for burn or stamps, newspapers, TV guides, a haircut, nail clippers. Trading or blagging burns (you don't pay double bubble for that) is a tricky business believe me and when you first come in everyone is blagging you for a burn, they know you have your smokers pack from Induction 1.

Picking your trading partners if you are giving them goods on a promise of the next canteen is another prison lottery. Some will honour the debt, some will forget or put it back another week telling you some Jackanory story. The last mentioned group will blank you or deny the agreement. Let it go is my advice, they will be unlikely to ask you again in the future — it's the one that got away it's not worth a ruck. TRUST!

As W Maree wrote in "Innocent as Sin" in *Prison Writing 2000*, "Time. It's all about time. A time to punish, punished by time …". I'm sat writing today, Day 14, having had some chronic personal time this morning while Dave Two went to the gym. I had a good trading session at association, swapping burn for more tea bags, whitener, sugar and … coffee, YYYEEEEEHHHAAAAA! What a great morning I got to smash myself in three times (some of my finest work) lay back smoked a burn and drank a fine sugary cup of coffee (first coffee for over two weeks) and dunked two custard creams. The Baclofen also has a bonus side effect of enhancing your boy glue moment … living the HMP X dream … for a lucky 20 minutes at least I must have had a horseshoe up my arse! The best day I've had in the first 14 days (each day is 86,400 seconds) and definitely not boring. As Luther Ingram once said,

If loving ME is wrong I don't wanna be right

or Teddy Pendergrass,

I've got so much love to give and I want to give it all to ME.

When it rains it pours. My ticket to torment has given me two letters through the cell door today, probation pre-sentence report video link interview at 10.30 am tomorrow and a letter from my little bro. He's the good looking one of the three of us boys. We have a little sister as well. I would never take a girl home if he was in as once they saw him they were full of, "Ahh he's lovely" and "How old is he again?". My wife was asked if she had married the right one on her hen do video, drunk, "It should have been the younger one hiccup!!" At my wedding my bros helped my best man with the speech, my little brother said in front of 170 guests,

"Congratulations to my brother on marrying Lisa" and to Lisa, "What are you doing?"

He's good as gold, his bender days are long gone, he's a stand up guy with two young boys, 18 months old and four months new. His missus is away for two weeks and he has the boys on his own. Now that's what I call a heavy sentence, a crucifying bit of bird!!

I expected some stick from him in the letter about my new home HMP X. He's reinforcing what I already know, good lad, he's laid it on a bit thick, but fair play I would have done the same. I'm trying hard to make sure I'm not doing it to you with LBP. Being banged up is prevention not cure, but for me it's a cure weirdly because of the drink, if it's drugs you're after you can find them banged up.

Am I an unrepentant addict or am I turning my life around? Only when I get back out will I know. I know I will need to prove that being good and going straight (drink and drugs and crime) can be better for me and my loved ones. Being banged up is certainly the worst thing. It's one big emotional roller coaster — some happy highs like today and some sad lows. You just have to ride it out, ride your bang up.

Writing LBP is my bird killer, being a sociable soul the bird succeeds in socially excluding me 22 hours a day. LBP is my sociable soul talking to you and later my family and loved ones as they are definitely doing my bird with me, no question about that. Ruth Wyner in *Prison Writing 2000* put that better than me in her contribution "The Festive Season in Prison" — thank you Ruth you are right. So in the boredom as I wait for liberty I can reinforce my mind to this bang up being my first and last and knowing that this is the point to turn away from drink and drugs and my destructive behaviour... You will make your own decision.

Day 15 today and a reminder of the prospect of my sentence from a video link to the probation service... the pre-sentence report. I'm in court on 25th Feb at the Crown Court in front of a judge to be sentenced. It's 60/40 on serving a custodial sentence which could be 18 months. I need to pray the judge got laid the night before, his shares have gone up in value and he's a morning person as it's a 9.30am appearance so at least I'm the first case of the day. If you assume you are serving time it will be a jackpot if you get a suspended sentence. I am playing both ends of course, me being me the Governor of HMP X has had a letter. I have called him over and spoken to him personally and will be handing him another letter tomorrow requesting a letter of support for my community service project. I will manage it myself, much better option than being in a charity shop. I'll end up smelling of old people.

Phone calls will give you a lifeline to the outside world, the credit is connected to your canteen sheet so takes a week to get onto your phone PIN (one of the few things on a canteen sheet that comes early!) I am forced to ration my calls to my daughter to once every three days until the canteen is rolling properly. Another bonus of HMP X is that I am getting on better with my wife than I had during the last six months. She knows where I am, she knows there will be no phone call from the police saying that I'm in a cell and not likely to turn up at four am wasted and needing to sleep on the sofa cause I've lost my keys again. In one week I lost two Blackberry Bolds (£400 each), a £1,400 Raymond Weil watch, a £400 Hugo Boss jacket and a £500 laptop — a bad manic week at the bender office.

You could try telephone sex to relieve the boredom but appreciate there's a queue of inmates behind you on the wing, I've never seen anyone trying yet. You could set a prison record or another sentence for indecent exposure. You could trade use of a mobile but if caught it will be more than your pants down it will be down the block and loss of privileges including the telly.

Smoking is probably the biggest pastime to relieve the boredom in HMP X. If you have burn it's always stashed about your person, down your sock, in your tucked in T-shirt, in your cell. If you're running low you're down to re-cycling your rusty nuts (rolly butts, dog ends). Every inmate bar one on my wing smokes. New inmates

69

who never smoked on the out begin to smoke. As I wrote in *Chapter 1* of LBP, a blag for a single cell is if you're a non-smoker as you're not allowed to be put in a cell with a smoker. From the minute the cell is opened on Golden Hour its every smoker for himself, the market is open. Some inmates are skilled fly-pitchers, hustling the burn from new inmates, old lags, people who owe them, people they owe. Even when other landings are unlocked and you're not even getting the door flap opened and banging on the door, trading can still be brokered through other inmates. Our doors and flap are blue, the small window gives you a slight view of three cells each side of the landing opposite to your cell. My third night inside an inmate peered through my flap and said,

"What's blue and pisses you off?"

"Don't know what."

He slammed the blue flap in my face … bastard.

I had little choice but to tick some burn at double bubble. Half an ounce borrowed means an ounce back … criminal! More exotic smoke is available but will cost you a half ounce of tobacco for one Jamaican Old Holborn. Other pills, thrills and bellyaches (as the Happy Mondays once said) are available but not at HMP X of course, just what I've heard from other prisons … safe bruv.

Story Book Dads is run through the library, an excellent idea — you read a story for your kids and it's recorded onto a CD and sound effects are added and it is sent home. It keeps a strong bond with your kids, they can hear your voice before bed according to the book on parent separation ... makes sense. I advise you to put your name down.

In my HMP X we have a wing for nonces, wronguns, kiddie fiddlers they are given a Karaoke session once a week on their association and this is referred to by the screws as the Gary Glitter Appreciation Society.

5.2 Food and Canteen

Well what more can I say about prison food: "Get in the queue before the health inspector" or "Hurry up before it gets warm"? You have probably heard the threat, "I hope you like hospital food" — well in your case I know you will eat prison food as it's this or nothing amigo. Prisoners will welcome every turkey twizzler Jamie Oliver had to offer, gladly.

When you first arrive and do Induction Phase 2, Day 2 you get to "feast your eyes" on the menu selection for the first time. It's another prison lottery literally you mark a line by the side of your choices (or chances more like: one of the soups I had at lunch was oxtail … tasted more like fox tail). It takes a week or so to get your selected menu (I know you're not surprised) so until then you are given "Chef's Choice" (whatever the chef has most of or whatever other prisoners don't choose). Do yourself a favour and hang around at the back of the queue, if you are the last landing to be sent down, you can choose from whatever is left, so you might get a choice.

Lunch at my new home comes around 12 noon (give or take). Dinner is around 5 pm-ish when you also get a breakfast pack including UHT milk, tea bags, whitener, sugar and jam sachets. No chance of a fry up here me old son although there's a rumour that Christmas Day you do get egg and bacon. In preparation for coming to HMP X I would start eating own brand cereals, Coco Pops, cornflakes, muesli and Weetabix. The prison versions are worse than own brand but it will be easier to get used to, if you know what I mean (Happy Shopper own brand by the way).

Don't ever go for a burger on the prison menu ever, you had your chance with the Reliance ride (see *Chapter 3*). I've never seen anything like it, picture the soles of your most worn out trainers dunked in the deep fat fryer of the dirtiest kebab house in your town … that's the prison burger … on its own … no bread roll, no lettuce, tomato, onion … it's a Burglar King.

In the police cells the veggie chilli was the best of a bad lot. In here I would try the veggie options, there's a bit more flavour and they have spices at least. In your trading try to get close to the servery staff, using LBP Rule 1: you'll get extra slops — sorry, spoonfuls — and might get the last of the loaf of bread, some extra slices included.

There's a scene in the film "Scum" where they are discussing the food with the chef and they complain about the battered fish being soggy. The chef says, "It's impossible to make crispy batter!" Well at HMP X it is impossible to get crispy batter or crispy chips.

When you're called down for a lunch and dinner with your plastic plate and bowl, take your time as it's valuable part of being out of your cell and trading. Keep your plate out when you move along the servery as you have an outside chance of extra scoops (because there is rarely a time when you finish lunch or dinner and feel full up). You need to make this hungry hole up with your canteen munchies.

When you arrive you get a bank account, if you read LBP you will be off and running in as little as three long, gruelling, stressed-out weeks. If like me you didn't know anything about anything and hadn't had an opportunity to read the LBP it takes four weeks.

On your canteen sheets you can order luxuries ... well basic luxuries ... it's not a Tesco or Asda list of goods, more Happy Shopper corner shop, but compared to prison basics it's a massive step up. Your essentials are telephone credit and burn (Don't forget to order Rizla if you're having the cheaper tobacco, a schoolboy error because the economy version comes without its own cigarette papers). Once these are covered you're going to have to pick carefully if you're up for a munchies binge: chocolate, crisps and sweets. If you want to rescue the flavourless prison food, your saviour will be brown sauce, mustard, salt and pepper. I would invest in vitamin supplements also as the prison diet is not covering your five a day. There's a lot of toothless prisoners in HMP X. I thought this was due to their violent past — now I think its scurvy due to the lack of vitamin C.

Day 20 today and I watched "Alien Two" last night, funny but the alien coming out of the bloke's stomach reminded me of the first few nights at HMP X. I wouldn't have been surprised to see one of those alien bastards coming through my guts (The combination of prison food and the major adjustment to prison, plus all the stress anxiety and despair that go with it). I thought I had worms for the first few days as I was constantly starving. I also had a glowing sensation in my belly due to the stress ... maybe they were glow worms!!

The meat in the sarnies and baguettes does look a little like the inner walls of the Queen Alien's lair. I'm sure there's more flavour in the film set than in the meat. Corned beef is what it is on the outside, smells like dog food and only Branston Pickle can save it, but the ham must be a typo on the menu sheet as its Spam not ham.

My digestion must be adjusting as I slept like a log last night, slowly becoming settled in HMP X … I wouldn't say comfortable, no chance. I'm waiting to get out of the cell. We have just come back from exercise. Dave Two stayed in the cell for some personal time. He looked white as a sheet when I came back and he is half cast!

I want to ring my daughter, I spoke to her days ago (due to my poxy phone credit), she was on the sofa and upset, missing a trip to a gallery with school. I queued for nearly half my association time yesterday (which was cut short cause they had no staff, this happens most weekends as all the screws want the weekend off) for the phone to make my call to her but by the time we were let out it was eleven am and when I called no-one answered. I am hoping to get out of my cell today, soon and call again. I hope she is there.

I am reading about separation and how it affects children, my wife always went crazy when I promised to see my daughter and then didn't turn up. This happened a lot toward the end of my bender, before I got remanded and fair play I knew my wife was right and this book confirms it's the worst thing you can do to a child is to let them down like that.

I can't tell my daughter exactly when I will call as the association is all over the Co-op. She goes to school at 8.30 am and we're supposed to get out during the week for Golden Hour at 8 am, but we're on the top floor and the screws are in no hurry. By the time I get up, get down and queue up with the second and third floor inmates it's another prison lottery and one I'm not winning as much as I'd like to. I would ring her before bedtime when I was on the outside but still separated. I miss doing that in here, but no chance until I get on education or a prison job, then its evening association.

HMP X hooch is another liquid refreshment for you but it's not on the canteen sheet, it's a cell made delight. You will need a litre bottle, an orange, some bread and some sugar. No exact quantities are required but peel the orange and squash the segments into the bottle, put in your sugar, squash your bread in and put the lid back on, then wrap the bottle in a towel or blanket to keep the concoction cosy.

Open the bottle every day to release the gases and after five days or so you have a hooch party waiting to happen … you can buy Rennies on the canteen sheet. I suggest you do before you drink your hooch as you're gonna need them.

I'm invited to an education forum group on Wednesday evening to discuss our ideas for future courses with the tutors. It's a bit tricky for me, I haven't been to any courses but am happy to go along for the coffee and biscuits and time out of the cell.

My eldest daughter will have to visit me soon as it has been a month since I have seen her — the longest we have ever been apart. When I was on self destruct benders I would not communicate with my family for up to eight days, then turn up looking like hammered shit, my young twins would not recognise me and my eldest daughter would ask where I had been and get upset. I would say I had been at work, my wife would get angry, what a twat I was, what a wanker, what a prick! I would rather be on a bender causing havoc, putting myself in harm's way, in police cells, in HMP X, than reading my girls a story before bed.

In my right mind now this can't be defended. My behaviour was selfish addiction, choosing to run away from my feelings, choosing drink and drugs over my wife and family. My wife has been a rock and has never spoken badly of me to my daughter — or about the way I have behaved. She has explained things to my daughter when she has been in floods of tears cause daddy didn't turn up AGAIN!: that sometimes Daddy makes the wrong decisions. If I'm staying at Her Majesty's pleasure after the 25th then she will visit and I will explain that this is where daddy is to help make the right decisions.

Jesus it's the hardest lesson, facing up to your weaknesses, your mistakes, on your own in HMP X — but when you have to explain it to a six year old girl who's as sharp as a Gillette Mach 7, as clever as a girl with three heads that you're a stupid man, that's a killer.

I can imagine it: "Yes darling Daddy decided to go out and drink himself stupid, take lots of cocaine, get arrested by policemen 25 times and end up in prison". The old parent rule, "Don't do as I do, do as I say" will come in handy when I get out and when the teenage years happen. All my girls are going to have a field day turning that one out on me ... Jesus I'll be like a lamb to the slaughter.

Mashed potato is lovely, it's the old instant stuff, Smash from the adverts. "For mash get Smash". They looked like metal versions of Zippy from Rainbow (If you don't remember forget about it). The mash is creamy, no lumps, hold the plate with both hands as the weight hits the plate hard from the ice cream scoop. Jacket potatoes are no good you've got more chance of laying an egg than getting a sunflower spread portion to melt into a jacket spud here, cold and soggy. New potatoes are a winner covered with butter and finished in the oven they are a rare treat (seen them once in 20 days). I also saw a tray of eggs for gammon — the eggs looked like the serving staff had laid them.

If you have a sweet tooth there are some things on offer. Yoghurts are winners, cakes and flapjacks are average, rice pudding and custard with tinned fruit in it, very average. Fruit, well oranges are useful for the hooch, bananas and apples are good. But the pièce de résistance is Saturdays when you get a pack of biscuits for lunch, so a cup of crap prison tea and a few dunked bikkies. It rocks!

Canteen orders never used to be so slow but recently the Prison Service has tried to make the canteen more efficient by making it worse for prisons and prisoners, excellent news. One prison is now responsible for canteen orders for all of the south east prisons. These orders are picked and packed by inmates who get paid £20 per week and have their hands on the store room keys. Of course these are trusted criminals, so the stock take is 100 per cent-ish.

Day 22 and my big dilemma yesterday was do I jump or stand firm and play another prison lottery? Dave Two was on his way to Milton Keynes as a Cat-C and I was hunting round for a new cell mate. Someone sound, I didn't want to end up with someone with hideous personal hygiene. I asked a fellow inmate or five if they knew anyone who was looking. Problems with this, I like the cell, it's warm, it's clean, I feel settled, and it's away from the association pool tables on the second floor. But it will turn into a living nightmare if I stay here and a new cell mate from hell turns up. Decisions, decisions. I have been offered to move across the landing, he is sound. I've had coffee, DVD player, burn and used his phone PIN but he's a player and as such has had a former cell mate smacked and another escorted out of the wing by armed security screws with helmets, truncheons and shields — they looked like the riot police. Hence he needs a cell mate.

Not only tricky as there are big pros and cons (he's a big con) but how to tell him "Thanks but no thanks" (nothing personal). I managed to politely explain that the cells on his side of the landing were dark and I needed the light. I think he knew I was backing off but he let me go. Celly number three came in after just three hours of having the place to myself. Three hours is a lot of personal time. I was white as a sheet. But I am not worried as some inmates get that they are chronic masturbators while banged up. I have no worries on this one I have always been a bear chronic self-abuser, I can't stop until there is only potato water coming out of the top of it. As my older brother would say, "It's like a Gurkha sword … once it's drawn it has to see blood".

Cell mate number three is Steve a seasoned veteran to bang up, he's 25 years new and been in and out constantly for the last five years, including three major prisons. Within the first few minutes sporting a black eye and fucked up shin I knew I had won the prison lottery. I would have to say he's the Ray Mears or Bear Grills of

HM prison system, well… much more knowledgeable of the system than my good self.

I have had another RESULT today. I came back from a health visit, which consisted of ten blokes marched to a large room, one inmate being seen in one hour then all sent back to the wing. I went through another wing where the pool tables had new cloth on them, the jammy bastards, ours are fucked. I remember being told not only am I in the worst prison but also on the worst wing. Final RESULT as I came back through to my wing, the table tennis bats and ball were out. I rushed the fella,

"Can I borrow those for association tomorrow?"

"No worries, sort him out bruv."

Excellent, table tennis tomorrow.

Getting back to prison food, it's fair to say that in the main it is part of the punishment, very, very rough justice being dished out. I caught three servery staff huddled round a pie singing "Happy Birthday to You", the pie was three that day. I risked the beef stew once. I was chewing on it for so long I started blowing bubbles!!

5.3 Application Forms and Letters

In HMP X you need to apply for everything, you can't take a crap without filling out an application form and getting it approved ... well not quite, but nearly. All apps have to be requested during Golden Time from the No 1 cleaner, who doesn't clean he looks after the stocks, supplies and paperwork you need. Once you have filled them in you give them to the screw to process — if it's not important enough to have its own box on the wing. Among other things, you need to apply for the following:

- jobs
- education
- additional phone numbers
- enhanced status
- emergency phone credit
- attending chapel
- visiting orders
- doctors
- CARAT referrals
- prison move requests
- accommodation (via BETA as they called it in HMP X, for the Benefits Education Training and Accommodation team. Get used to the shorthand in your prison)
- complaints

- haircut.

When filling in forms check with the screw that they are filled in properly, it takes weeks to process forms as it is and if anything is wrong with them they won't tell you, you simply won't get a response.

When you arrive in prison your status is "standard". If you misbehave it is likely to be reduced to "basic". If you follow the rules of LBP, before you know what is happening it will be "enhanced" and life more comfortable.

You get two second class letters a week courtesy of HMP X. This includes the envelopes and the prison paper stamped HMP X, lovely for the misses, my mum or my nan! Think about it though when was the last time you wrote a letter? You know, wrote with a pen and paper and your hand. When was the last time you received a letter from a loved one? All the post I ever get is either junk mail, the bank telling me I'm over my overdraft, or from credit card companies, debt collection agencies and that's about it. Letters are an outdated medium, it can all be done by txt, email and social networking sites (Okay Facebook...I didn't want to say it, it's a stalkers paradise!). The feeling of expressing yourself to your missus or mum with a pen and paper is a powerful one. You connect with the addressee more than any other way, the oldest way and still the best and in this day and age the most unique but also the simplest.

You have to leave the envelope open and the screws may read through your letter (they screen around five per cent). If you're a PPO (prolific persistent offender) they will screen all of yours, not me and hopefully not you (PPOS don't need the LBP they have helped me write it). In prison many of the population can't read and write, and around half of those I met had only a basic knowledge of either. Some inmates have nothing to say and can't be arsed to write letters and then moan that they don't get any. I would say the least tradeable commodity is stamps, paper and envelopes.

My new celly reckons he has got so used to the format of putting his name and prison number on the back of the envelope that he now does it on the outside and posts his letters with the envelope open ... that's institutionalised ... I don't think the postman bothers to screen five per cent ... unless they are birthday cards with cash in ££.

The letters you write not only help make sense of your predicament but also help you to come to terms with ending up at HMP X. The letters you write out also equate with how many letters you get back — and believe me receiving contact and support from the outside world and in letter form is better than a phone call by a mile. A phone call is great but is finished the moment the handset is down, a letter gives you time and messages sink in, its personal and private and the feelings and thoughts sink deep as you read them over again and again.

If you don't have anyone to write to send letters to departments of the prison, prison support groups, check out *Inside Time* the free newspaper for prisoners, your local shop, your local pub, anywhere you can remember the address of and anyone you may have an outside chance of getting a £10 postal order from. Look after the canteen pennies and the pounds will get you some burn/phone credit/vitamins/coffee, etc... Good luck.

5.4   Medication

If like me your new home is due to mental health problems fed by excessive drink and drugs use then you are sure to be clucking in the first few weeks of your bird. I have mentioned how I managed to get Baclofen sorted in the Doctor Blag section (see *Chapter 2.4*), but that has now gone sideways and the head nurse, who as you know has got no real motivation to help, just quotes the British Medical Council. I ran out of my prescription and spoke to the nurse at the counter on our wing. She requested an appointment with the doctor but the doctor has been sacked so the senior nurse (a tosser and no mistake) would not prescribe as he feared being prosecuted. Jesus, a chicken licken approach to his job, I thought they were trying to help people especially in here. I know I told you about this earlier but it winds me up.

Anyway meds are distributed three times a day: Golden Hour, lunch and dinner. You're likely to miss exercise if you are on the top floor, the queue for meds is long. Eighty per cent of prisoners take drugs on the outside (I couldn't comment on the inside). Your fellow inmates in the queue for meds will be arguing about upping their dosage, extra pills that they have missed, any blag to get some more meds (can't blame them for trying, but this is the only time they can try so fair play). But during Golden Hour you need to be in three places at once. It's a prison lottery! Its 8 am for fucks sake, you're half asleep — they are usually late getting out so trying to get your brain in gear is hard work especially when you've had a prison night's sleep. So with a queue of arguing, half asleep smack rats clucking it takes a while. Lunch is easier as its meds queue first then lunch queue itself, the lottery is if they are running out of food you might get caught short … what's more important meds or food … the eternal question?

Dinner is another game of chance. If you get the food first then join the queue for meds the food could be cold before you get back to your cell, if meds first they might run out of some of the grub if you're on the top floor like me, good luck fella. Your medication may be your choice, for me it's the food, not being a true drug addict.

Get your appointment in for sleeping pills, its hard work getting your head down in prison in the first few weeks. It's much harder to ride out your bang up and trade on the landings. If you don't get your sleep, trading will be one way traffic, if you snooze you lose. It's going to take weeks to get in front of the doctor if your HMP X has one — ours has gone of course — it will help big time.

My court appearance is tomorrow. I tried to get in touch with my wife, the phone queue was massive and 15 minutes later I got to ring the landline. She was on the phone so it went to answerphone. I left a message asking her to come to court with the twins. I want her to whisper "Daddy" to the girls so they can call out in the court. But who listens to voicemail messages on the landline! and I'm banged up for the rest of the day cause there has been a stabbing on another wing. On top of that I can hear the table tennis bats and ball downstairs ... Oh the humanity!!

5.5 Clothes

I love my clothes. I have a business wardrobe and a casual one, lots of trainers, shoes, suits and jackets, on most days I will change at least twice a day. In bang up I'm changing twice a week into the same grey and burgundy pyjamas/tracksuit (excuse for). I've been in the same pair of trainers for four weeks. They are put on the window sill at night to air out. Jesus there's pairs of trainers I don't wear for a month, but those I am wearing now can walk to lunch and association by themselves.

You start with two pairs of blue boxers, two pairs of socks, two burgundy T-shirts, two grey flannel tracksuit bottoms, two grey flannel tracksuit tops and that ... is ... it AAAAGGGHHHHHAAA! Mate what a state, I look like I'm walking around in grey pyjamas nearly as old as me, I look like a criminal. Walking around five star offices in a good suit with silk lining to the ankle makes you feel a million bucks! Walking around in an oversized hamster cage dressed like this I feel about £1.26 pence. You're not alone. The majority of the first timers or skint three time losers are wearing the same. On the outside as on the inside it's all about status, clothes maketh the man. The longer term inmates or enhanced inmates are wearing jeans, T-shirts, jumpers and I am sure they feel a bit more human, not just a number. The trouble is all clothes in here have to be bought through catalogues and if like me you came in skint and you have no money being sent in you're in trouble ... or so I thought.

Your sacred trainers can be sent in but only within the first 28 days of being in HMP X. If you're on remand you can arrange for your own clothes to be bought in on a visit. You need to get an app from the No 1 cleaner and describe in detail the clothes that they are bringing in for you. You can have:

- seven pairs of socks and boxers
- three pairs of jeans
- three pairs of trainers
- three T-shirts
- three jumpers
- three tracksuits.

I would not advise suits, ties and shoes, no use to no one in here.

The app needs to go to the SO (senior officer) via your PO (personal officer) 48 hours before the visit. You have to be enhanced status in some cases six weeks, in my case eight weeks … another beast! (You also can't have them brought in on a Sunday).

A few days after the visit your clothes will arrive and — not that I have had the luxury of wearing my clothes in here — it will help your bird in terms of comfort, confidence and status. If I had known this I would have had my Hugo Boss, Armani, Ralph Lauren and Paul Smith. I am getting upset thinking about this section, I am sinking into a pit of despair, there is a huge, heavy prison between me and my wardrobe … AARRGGHHHH.

But you're in the same boat as most in the prison attire as long as you're not an attempted escapee (as I said, there's always someone worse off). He will have to wear a pair of trousers with patches of yellow and greenish blue, and a top with patches, a full on clown suit. They only get one set of these and they get it taken off them at night and given back in the mornings.

6 Getting On with Your Bird

6.1 Education

In a previous brief stage of my career I sold academic qualifications into the Prison Service (via NOMS, the National Offender Management Service), a year on I am here at Her Majesty's pleasure going through the process as a consumer. Unbelievable and yes you guessed it, to get onto education you have to fill in an app to BETA. You've already requested it at induction but keep sending the apps to nudge things along.

The first part of the process is to establish your English and Maths levels. The education room has computers and the tests for both are completed on these. The minute I got in front of the keyboard and screen I was off onto a web browser and tried to get into my business servers to access my emails ... more chance of laying an egg ... the world loves a trier and I am very trying indeed so my wife says, but she was warned by all my friends and family about that when we first met. She didn't listen of course.

Women are funny fellas, we went to salsa lessons once to spend some time together. A friend of mine said, "Salsa lessons ... that's one step away from marriage guidance ...". We later tried marriage guidance, she had more moves in that arena! Being banged up has helped us to stop fighting at least.

My wife told me I had a call from a mate who looks after my email domains saying he was taking me to court if I didn't pay him. She said I was already at HMP X and he then said to send me his best and he was sorry, we can deal with it when I'm out ... bless him.

The tests were like being back at school, the questions were tedious and the sums were back to algebra and trigonometry, reminded me of schools, old school friends and past girls, especially my wife back in the time warp twilight zone as it was 20 years ago when I sat exams for GCSE.

You can take courses from IT and Web Design to Creative Writing or Starting a Business. Minimal courses on offer at my HMP X as it is a holding prison, when you are shipped out to a real prison once sentenced there are more options open to you in terms of vocational qualifications, like tree surgery and for electricians, builders and plumbers. Courses will give you a weekly income, more time in the gym, longer days as you're occupied with the course and your association is in the early evening after dinner. You'll also get paper for letters and for writing your own LBP if you feel the urge. Everybody has a story to tell. Work books can be requested from your tutors a few times over. My new celly, Steve has achieved a few diplomas at GCSE level in Web Design and IT. I need to get in front of a computer to type out LBP before the closing dates of the Koestler Awards (which have a section for Non-fiction Creative Writing). I had a visit from a BETA screw today who had received my letter sent to the No1 Governor for my community service project, the wrong department had received the letter but this is being faxed to my solicitor by BETA and will show that I'm being pro-active in wanting to be released.

I also wrote to BETA to offer to help with their Starting a Business Programme called "Going Solo". I have had no reply but again it was someone to write to. My business development experience and masters degree must have made them think "Sod this smart arse".

6.2 Work

There are two types of employment available in HMP X: working for the prison or working for outside companies that use prison labour. If you want to work for the prison you have a few different choices. All come with perks of the job, time out of cell and better gym sessions (if they remember to come and get you). As my HMP X is a holding prison the wages are poor compared to real prisons.

Food Servery – The most sought after job in the prison, if you ever go into the cell of a servery worker you will see the perks with your own eyes … food, glorious food … you never see a skinny servery worker. The way to a man's heart is through his stomach, the extra helpings cover you from every angle, you're a grade A trader and no mistake. Likelihood of getting a servery job is low, the queue is longer than for medication in Golden Hour.

Gym Orderly – The second most sought after job in the prison, size matters in terms of status in prison and these boys are training every day. Everyone wants more gym and the orderlies can slip you out of your cell and onto gym lists. Again this gives you major trading currency on the wing but the waiting list for gym orderly is nine months, so I hear.

Library Assistant – A useful job if you want a more civilised environment to work in, it also gives you an angle as you are responsible for all newspapers and the weekly TV guides. You also get first pick of the books and can help prisoners to read and to write letters. Rare to get jobs coming up in the library … there's a pattern forming here isn't there.

Health Care Orderly – A unique opportunity but you are detached from the main body of inmates, so not so many trading opportunities. However your cell is bigger than the No 1 Governor's office and you're surrounded by nurses, admin staff and orderlies and have keys to the medicine cupboard (only joking). You're more likely to see Portsmouth Football Club get back in the Premiership than get this job.

No 1 Cleaner – You never actually have to do any cleaning, you are in charge of the six wing cleaners, the cleaning products for prisoners and all the apps. You get a single cell but your trading calibre is lower than Gym or Servery as the prison issue toiletries are very average. The last No 1 was in the job for 18 months … hopefully you're not in prison for that long.

Reception Orderly – You're the friendly face of HMP X as new inmates arrive (if they didn't chance on the screws in a good mood). They will fleece new inmates at induction for a few burns and do have access to the smokers packs store. Again, a single cell but you need to be in HMP X for sometime before they let you lose on bending new prisoners heads. The best wages in this HMP X, £18 due to the long shifts, not quite open all hours but close.

Laundry – The lower end of the job scale you will get access to wash your own clothes or trade with senior inmates who want their clothes washed. Will get you a single cell if one is available. Washing powder trading makes you unique, you can buy it on the canteen sheet but few inmates do.

Cleaner – The good news is you're out of your cell all day, the bad news is you're pushing a broom and a mop around. For me prison is bad enough without your head being down pushing a broom or mop, I would feel worse not better. You can act as a runner between cells, so will do favours and win friends as you are out of the cell all day. They walk around like John Wayne of course due to all the personal time.

You have to bear in mind how many jobs there are compared to the volume of inmates, the odds can be as high as 40-1 against you getting a job in some prisons. Just keep sending apps and nudging the senior officer as they send them over to the allocations department. There is still a big recommendation from existing workers that can affect things, so get friendly with the staff within the departments you are looking to work in. Another HMP lottery awaits ...

Outside company opportunities will depend on the type of prison, you and the economic climate. Currently we have assembly lines for companies in light electrical and computer repairs. Again you're getting more liberty, getting paid and may have the opportunity of getting friendly with the company representative and obtaining a job on the outside, or building a skill to use on the outside. Anything to keep your brain occupied is worth doing.

6.3   Going to Court — Sentence

My solicitors sent a letter with the list of charges and a court date of 25th Feb and I was looking down the list, shaking my head as I remembered each arrest and the statements read out to me by the interviewing officers. I sunk down the chair, further each time hoping the trap door would open, what the fuck was I thinking and saying?!

I had been Pub Watched from my area and barred from most of the pubs in it. In addition, every Fuller's pub on the south coast, a direct order from head office. The two local hotels, a string of curry houses and takeaways, the two local taxi firms, two local off-licences, the local Tesco superstore, two holiday camps and a hairdressers. Good friends were now not letting me past the front door, making lame excuses about going out or having dinner. You could see they were very wary of me and my behaviour. Another good friend didn't invite me to his baby's christening (I turned up anyway) because he said he didn't know which Frankie was going to turn up the Jekyll or the Hyde (on a manic bender or sober). Invites for my wife and I were now addressed only to my wife ... Jesus!

On the day of the court hearing you are picked up by the Reliance boys and girls. A screw comes to the cell and gets you up, you pack all your belongings, for me a plastic folder with letters and paperwork and the manuscript of LBP. On Friday the 25th Feb no one came for me, I was gutted. All over the weekend I was left to stew and wonder why I didn't go to court. Had there been additional charges? I could be re-remanded, my solicitors and the judge couldn't make sense of all the charges as there were so many. I couldn't clearly remember, being so out of my box, the cell with two plug sockets was getting smaller.

I received a letter on the Monday apologising, saying the hearing had been moved to Friday 4th March (I was unhappy but relieved). The following Thursday I could not help but think about getting out, a 60/40 chance. If the judge was in a good mood and got laid the night before and the sun was shining it could be a suspended sentence. Friday 4th March and no screw came to the cell to collect me, fuck a duck I could hear them calling other prisoners but not me. Bastards!! I rang the alarm button in the cell, You're told it's for emergencies only, this was in that category for me. A screw came.

"What's the emergency?"

I flashed the solicitor's letter.

"I'm due in court gov."

"Not according to my list."

The flap shut in my face. Fuck two ducks another weekend of wondering began, but was cut short as when I rang the enemy (her indoors, the trouble and strife) she said I was due in court Wednesday next week. My roast chicken leg (sparrow's leg), soggy potato wedges and overcooked carrots went down badly that Sunday. I could have been round the family table eating leg of lamb, mint sauce, roast parsnips, apple pie and custard. (Gutted).

Tuesday morning a day before the hearing a screw came to the door and said, "Court today Owens, get up." What the fuck is going on now! Well at least a day early is better than being pushed back again. I was ready in ten minutes, chained smoked knowing I'd have no chance of a smoke all day. Some inmates will stash burn and matches but you have to be in the shit if you're smoking "Rusty Sheriffs Badge" or "Brown Starfish" a variety not for me bruv (no prizes for guessing where they stash it).

Into the court suit, crumpled to pieces since I left it on 1st Feb. I requested a trouser press. The screw looked shocked and smiled.

"Knowing these bloody pen pushers we'll have one soon."

"Yeah," I replied, "but I bet it will be broken."

No new van this time, a tiny box with double plastic tinted windows and a moulded plastic chair (not unlike the metal detector chair in reception). Inmates left the prison like battery chickens travelling to the Crown Court slaughter house. Better food and coffee at the courthouse, I was cuffed and brought into the interview room to meet my barrister. Very attractive lady, a pleasant surprise, in her sexy tones she explained the lottery, as she put it,

"You're stood on a trap door and the judge is holding the lever."

Wonderful, just what I expected and well put. I'm sure in Frankie Land she undressed and tied me to the table with just her grey wig and suspenders on shouting, "Take me, Take me".

On getting into the dock, surrounded by safety glass I saw my wife, younger sister and dad. My wife blew me a kiss, I mouthed "Hello" to all three and faced the judge. I don't think he'd been laid, I'm sure he had piles, shit he had both hands on the lever!!

Within a minute I was back in the holding cell, the judge had flicked through the papers and said there were two outstanding issues. Fuck three ducks and chuck in a couple of swans into the bargain, this can't be happening. Another hour and a half in the holding cell, what the fuck was it now. Finally I was collected and taken back up to court, the charges were read out along with statement snippets, only the worse bits, I was sinking again, the crack in the trapdoor was getting wider.

I had gone guilty on everything and written a letter to the judge (make sure you write one it only helps) so no jury, just Judge Grumpy Bollocks. My barrister presented my side of the story, my fall from grace, but it was clear Judge Sad Sack had made up his mind up. He had decided it was to be custodial sentence.

He read each of the charges and gave me a sentence in weeks: four weeks plus four weeks plus four weeks, plus four weeks plus six weeks plus six weeks, plus 12 weeks plus 26 weeks plus 52 weeks. If you've seen the film "Stir Crazy", Richard Prior and Gene Wilder are sentenced and Prior starts screaming, "WHA, WHA, WHA". That was me that was! My arse was going 20 pence 50 pence as I added up the weeks: 118 weeks in total, two years, three months and two weeks, "WHA, WHA, WHA" the drop from the trapdoor was much longer than I expected, I needed a fuckin parachute.

"Take him down" (I'm already at the bottom of my cage Fucko).

I waited in the holding cell, hold on did he say … concurrent or consecutive … ?

Barrister beautiful met me again and said, "It's a year, serve six months" — a gift from the gods. I had already served over a month, four and a half left and maybe an option for a tag for three months, could be as little as six weeks ... but he could have let me walk, some you win and some you lose.

It felt like lose then lose then win then lose ... grumpy justice!

6.4 Never Going Back

Now for the final scribble from my LBP pencil and scrappy paper on what I hope will be helpful to new-inmates and their loved ones. For me I'm convinced that this is the experience that will get me back on the rails and help me lead a better life again. Prison isn't just shit its dog shit and it isn't just normal dog shit it is the white crumbling old dog shit. It was never my ambition to go to prison, hurt my wife and family, push my friends away, blow up a great job opportunity but I made it all happen, Me myself and I.

There are a few more months to wait in prison, but the time is going quicker now and I'm a working man. I have the library assistant job and start my IT course next week. Like buses these things all come at once: two days ago my detox course was offered to me as well. I have been notified of my Category also, now I am C-Cat, next stage will be allocation to a prison to serve out my sentence. Hilarious as the Cat form said I had been allocated to HMP OVERCROWDING!!!...I had to check if this was a real prison ... it's not.

Things are becoming easier, the roller coaster of highs and lows is slowing down, I am learning not to be so hard on myself and not to be a prisoner of my past. Future freedom is the focus. I wanted to be a writer and journalist as a child and grew up in hospitality, this misadventure has allowed me to write LBP which is designed to help people, the mantra of hospitality. Being in prison writing LBP has re-kindled my passion for the pen and getting down my thoughts on paper.

The prison life is bearable if it is going to serve a purpose, have an outcome, serving time for me had the following positives:

- forty-six days clean of drink and drugs (great head start for getting out)
- healthier looking (all those early nights!)
- lost weight and the double chin (result!)
- wrote *The Little Book Prison*.

I'm not going to list the negatives ...the LBP would turn into a trilogy!!. I have behaved like a loser and the worst thing is I'm a bad loser ... an alcoholacaust has taken place and no mistake.

Serving time for time's sake is retribution not rehabilitation (thank you Mr. Archer). It's a waste of my precious years at nearly 37 (I will be spending my 37th birthday at HMP X). There's no new experiences in here of any worth, once you have learned the ropes you are just burning time. I hope you are burning weeks not months or months not years.

You're three times more likely to go back to prison once you've been inside, so don't be one of those. Have a good time all the time, remember, "If you can't do the time, don't do the crime".

Index